MW01079153

The
Discerning of
Spirits

FRANK HAMMOND

THE DISCERNING OF SPIRITS

BY FRANK HAMMOND

ISBN 10: 0-89228-368-8
ISBN 13: 978-089228-368-2

IMPACT CHRISTIAN BOOKS, INC.

332 Leffingwell Ave., Suite 101
Kirkwood, MO 63122

WWW.IMPACTCHRISTIANBOOKS.COM

All scripture quotations are from the King James Version of the Bible unless otherwise noted.

Scripture quotations identified NASB are from the New American Standard Bible® (NASB), Copyright © 1960, 1962, 1963, 1968, 1971, 1972, 1973, 1975, 1977, 1995 by The Lockman Foundation. Used by permission. www.Lockman.org.

The Discerning of Spirits

When God calls us into ministry, whatever that ministry is, God equips us. This is a fundamental principle in the way God works in our life.

God has called all of us into spiritual warfare and spiritual battle. His Church will be a militant Church, and the gates of hell shall not prevail against her. I say this to encourage you in two ways. First, so that you would know your potential in the Body of Christ, that you can be equipped by the Holy Spirit to face whatever challenges are in your life, or in your family. Second, I encourage you that the gates of hell are real, the enemy is real and therefore spiritual warfare is real. God has given this ministry of spiritual battle not just to me, Frank Hammond, or to my wife Ida Mae, but to you. You are a soldier, and because God has called you to be a soldier, he wants to equip you with spiritual armor and spiritual weapons.

Every believer should be involved in spiritual battle. Let's take a quick look at this commission to warfare in Scripture to back this point up.

In Matthew 10, Jesus commissioned the twelve disciples to go out and to minister.

> **And when he had called unto him his twelve disciples, he gave them power against unclean spirits, to cast them out, and to heal all manner of sickness and all manner of disease.**

What is the first task Jesus gives his disciples in this commission? He gave them power against unclean spirits. He says "I give you power," and this is power over unclean spirits to cast them out. So, the twelve went with the authority that God had given them and they accomplished that ministry that God had assigned them.

The identical thing happened in the 10th chapter of Luke where Jesus commissioned the seventy disciples. How do we know? Because the first thing they reported back to Jesus was that demons were subject to them:

> **And the seventy returned again with joy, saying, Lord, even the devils are subject unto us through thy name.**

Again, the power and authority required for the ministry of deliverance were given to Jesus' followers as He commissioned them. We are not told of a special ceremony or event that took place in order for this commission to be valid. All we are told in Scripture is that the Lord commissioned His followers. Why? Because the power and authority was already resident in His name.

Now pay special attention to this. Later on, in Mark 16:15–17, Jesus gave the same commission to the entire church:

> **And he said unto them, Go ye into all the world, and preach the gospel to every creature... And these signs shall follow them that believe; In my name shall they cast out devils**

First the twelve, then the seventy, and now the entire Church is being inducted into God's fight against demons. What are we to conclude from these three commissions? Simply that every believer should be involved in spiritual battle in some form or fashion. You are a soldier by virtue of your citizenship in the Kingdom of God. He didn't just send out one squad of the church to do a work of deliverance here and there. He sent 100% of the twelve, and 100% of the seventy and finally 100% of His Church to the ministry of casting out demons.

All of us should be involved in the ministry of deliverance in some fashion. When God calls, He equips!

DEMONSTRATIONS OF THE POWER TO CAST OUT DEMONS

We read in the first chapter of Mark, where Jesus went into the synagogue. There was a man present who disrupted the meeting under the power of an unclean spirit. Jesus rebuked that spirit and commanded it to leave him.

Now the scribes and the Pharisees who were gathered in the synagogue that day were amazed at what took place! They knew about evil spirits. They had methods that they employed to deal with evil spirits, but they had never seen such authority. They looked at each other and said "what thing is this? What kind of new doctrine are we being introduced to here?" "This man Jesus doesn't use incantations, he doesn't use gimmicks in order to get spirits out of people. He just speaks to them. He speaks with the word of authority."

Jesus has given us the same power and the authority to deal with evil spirits that He demonstrated in the synagogue that day. And this episode, in the synagogue, began first and foremost with Jesus *discerning* an evil spirit in the man.

In the eighth chapter of Acts, it speaks of the ministry of Philip, the evangelist. It says in verse 5–7:

> Then Philip went down to the city of Samaria, and preached Christ unto them.
>
> And the people with one accord gave heed unto those things which Philip spake, hearing and seeing the miracles which he did.
>
> For unclean spirits, crying with loud voice, came out of many that were possessed with them: and many taken with palsies, and that were lame, were healed.

What a fascinating evangelism technique! It says in the NASB about the crowd Philip was preaching to: "the crowds with one accord were giving attention to what was said by Philip." Why? Because they saw the miracles that Philip was performing under the anointing of the Holy Spirit. They saw the "signs that he performed" and as a result they listened intently to him. The first miracle mentioned that they saw was deliverance, the casting out of demons. Evil spirits were crying out and leaving people, and the torment of those people was ended. Miracles are not natural happenings, they are supernatural happenings. They were witnessing a supernatural miracle of deliverance. Philip was moving in the gifts of the Spirit and lives were being forever changed. He was equipped for the ministry God called him to.

The apostle Paul says in 1st Corinthians, in paraphrase, "I didn't come before you with eloquent speech and such tactics. I was feeble in that department. But I, Paul, did come to you in a demonstration and in the power of God's Holy Spirit." So when Paul went out to minister, he was equipped by God. He wasn't trying to convince people intellectually. It was a spiritual manifestation that followed Paul, and the Holy Spirit was coming with power, and with convicting miracles to back him up.

Paul was ministering by the inspiration and the power and the authority of the Spirit of God. And that is what God has called us to do, to minister in that same fashion.

To repeat, when God calls you to do something, He equips you to do it. You may not be in the forefront, you may not be in front of people leading and teaching every day about warfare and the ministry of deliverance, but God has a place for you in the ranks of His army. And if you will find that place, and fill that place, you can know *with confidence* that God has an equipping for you. He will give you all that you need. God has commissioned the whole church to warfare.

Let me give you a personal example of this in my life. When God called me to preach I said, "Oh, God I can't do that! I don't know how to stand up in front of people. I'm scared and it makes me nervous when I stand up in front of two or three people and try to express myself." I was so timid and shy; I felt inferior in my abilities. I didn't even know whether I had anything to say if I did stand up in front of people. Nevertheless, I obeyed God. Even though it was torturous to begin with, to go against all the oppression that the enemy was throwing against me, I found out that God equipped me for what he wanted me to be and what he wanted me to do.

Along those lines, Ida Mae used to ask me "why do you sound like the last preacher you heard preach?" You see, I would listen to other preachers and then I would imitate them hoping to be successful. Then I learned that all I had to be was just brother Frank! Thank God I don't have to be somebody else; I can be who Christ made me to be.

FUNDAMENTAL PRINCIPLES OF WARFARE

I want to lay down a few fundamental premises, on the subject of the equipping of the saints. I am talking to you as a deliverance people, whom God has called into spiritual warfare and called into spiritual battle. If I will do what He has called me to do, and stay within the limits and the boundaries of that, then I will have my reward and so will you. The first premise that we have already seen, is that God equips us for service. The second principle I want you to lay hold of is that God awards us not based on our successes but according to our faithfulness. He wants all of us to be faithful to our calling. And everyone has the same basic calling as expressed through the commission to the Church mentioned earlier. It is, generally speaking, as we move into this broad commission that we find our specific, unique ministry.

The next principle I want you to lay hold of is in second Corinthians 10, where it says:

> **"For the weapons of our warfare are not carnal, but mighty through God to the pulling down of strong holds..."**

This is another premise, a foundational principle I want you to lay firm hold on, because it is vital to what God's Spirit is saying to us in this hour. The weapons we use in spiritual battle are not fleshly or carnal weapons. They are instead mighty, supernatural weapons from God. They are mighty because they are divinely bestowed, spiritual weapons. The weapons of our warfare are not carnal!

You cannot fight the devil with carnal weapons. You cannot, for instance, use your fist and punch him or his demons in the nose. We have to instead use the weapons that God has made available to us, and know that they are mighty indeed. They are effective. They will work!

Fleshly weapons are not effective against the devil, only the weapons God has supplied are effective. Right in line with that principle, in Ephesians 6, Paul says we "wrestle not against flesh and blood but against principalities and powers." Our warfare is not against fleshly beings, despite the enemy's attempt to convince us otherwise. Our battle is against spiritual forces at work in people's lives.

Paul says to put on the whole armor of God, the complete armor of God, that you may stand against the "wiles of the devil." The equipment that God gives to us is not lacking; we do not have a partial, limited amount of armor, but we have a full armor. We have all that we need in the battle against the hosts of hell.

A verse that gave me great comfort when I first started out in the deliverance ministry was Luke 10:19. I was so fearful of the enemy's retaliation! But then the Lord spoke this verse to me, and it settled deep in my soul:

> **Behold, I give unto you power to tread on serpents and scorpions, and over all the power of the enemy: and nothing shall by any means hurt you.**

Never again, from that point onwards, did I have any fear of the enemy's power. Jesus told us that we can tread upon the enemy, even the serpents and scorpions of the demonic kingdom, and nothing shall hurt us.

THE GIFTS OF THE SPIRIT ARE GOD'S EQUIPPING

Now the gifts of the Holy Spirit represents God's empowerment to us, as believers. In first Corinthians 12, beginning in verse seven, there comes a listing of the gifts of the spirit. You see when God says he empowers us, that is not something nebulous, it's not something indefinite. God has presented to us specific channels through which His power will flow. There are avenues through which His Holy Spirit will operate. And here, in 1 Cor. 12, He begins to mention these channels and avenues. They are distributed by the Spirit and they are for the benefit of everyone who is involved, every member of the body of Christ.

The first two gifts listed are the *word of wisdom* and the *word of knowledge*. Next we find the gifts of *faith* and *healing*, then *miracles* and *prophecy*, *discerning of spirits*, *tongues* and *interpretation of tongues*. If you count all of those there are nine supernatural gifts of the Holy Spirit. Let me say this again, these are the channels by which the Holy Spirit's power and authority comes into our life as we are baptized in the Holy Spirit. We become a spiritually equipped, supernaturally endowed believer. It is through these gifts that we are empowered to do the ministry and the work of God, His great commission.

Right in the middle of that listing is the gift of the *discerning of spirits*. This is one of the main gifts needed for casting out demons and the ministry of deliverance. It is a powerful weapon that is most needed in the ministry of spiritual warfare. We must earnestly desire the operation of that gift!

THE HOLY SPIRIT AND NOTHING ELSE

Here is another premise. We must rely upon the Holy Spirit for the ministry of deliverance and nothing else. We must not lean upon our own understanding, we must not lean upon the arm of the flesh, or the voice of demons, but we must learn to rely completely on the Holy Spirit to empower us and to guide us in all that we do in deliverance and spiritual warfare. Why? Because if we attempt to minister deliverance without the gifts of the Spirit, and the empowerment thereof, then it will not be long until we resort to the flesh for our help. Here is where my conviction rests.

Somebody asked me once, "Brother Frank, when you begin to minister to someone with the problem of schizophrenia, as described in *Pigs in the Parlor*, with what demon do you always start?" I said "I don't start with any particular demon, because the ministry depends on a case-by-case basis, and I have to rely on the Holy Spirit for every case."

Every case of deliverances is separate. You can write something down and say here's the format that I will follow. But when we rely on formula we are not listening to the Holy Spirit, and we will miss a lot of the things that God wants to say to us and show us. We are tying our hands by tradition and not listening to the guidance of the Holy Spirit.

What I'm trying to say is this: become dependent upon the Holy Spirit! Don't become dependent upon past ways of success or anything else. Make the decision, commit to the fact that you are going to follow the Spirit each time you minister. Because if you don't, you will become dependent upon fleshly ways, in a sense eating "yesterday's manna." The things God gave for yesterday's ministry were good, just like the manna received by the Israelites in the wilderness. However, one day it was good but the next day it was filled with worms and stank.

As a side note, I have seen a lot of fleshly things done in the name of deliverance. I went to minister to a 12-year-old girl not long ago, and when the mother brought the girl for ministry, she wanted to know before we started ministering "now how are *you* going to do this?" She was very cautious. She said the last time she took her daughter to a deliverance minister, when she got home "her daddy was very upset." I asked "why was her daddy upset?" "Well," she said, "she was bruised all over her body." I said "how on earth did that happen?" "Well," she said "the deliverance ministry I went to explained to us that certain demons indwell certain areas of the body and the way to get them out was to pound on that part of the body. And so they had pounded on her legs and her back, and when she got home she had bruises." This is a completely unacceptable, and entirely flesh-based (e.g. carnal) form of ministry. I feel it is important to tell you some of the things that we have encountered when people have moved away from God's Spirit and into the flesh in order to administer deliverance.

I have heard of instances where, when faced with difficulty getting a demon out of somebody, the minister will grab the communion wine and pour it down the person's throat. They are resorting not to the word of authority, not to the empowerment of the Holy Spirit, but to fleshly and carnal means.

We were in a conference several years ago in Pennsylvania. Evil spirits took over a young man in the back of the auditorium. He was a young man in his early 20s, and he was completely taken over by evil spirits and thrown to the floor. Ida Mae made her way to the back of the auditorium to see if she could help, as there were not many counselors in that meeting. By the time she arrived at the back of the room, she could not even see the young man because he was covered up with Bibles. Everybody around him had thrown their Bibles on top of Him! You know the word of God is the "sword of the spirit," right? Yes, but not in this manner. I have seen people trying to get the devil out of somebody by laying a Bible on their head, or on their chest. This is a fleshly error. Saints, the way you use the Word of God is to quote the word of God. Let the sword of the Spirit come out of your mouth: "thus saith the Lord!" That's what Jesus did. He did not throw a scroll at the devil during the wilderness temptation. He quoted Scripture. If we don't, we are apt to fall into fleshly methods.

I've seen ministers lay crucifixes on people, spin rosary beads; all sorts of things. I've even heard people do a ritual chanting of the blood. "The blood, blood, the blood, the blood, etc." Now the Scripture says we overcome him, the devil, by the blood of the Lamb. But you use the weapon of the blood by telling the devil what the blood of Jesus does, not by chanting it! "The blood of Jesus has justified this man! The blood of Jesus sanctifies this man! The blood of Jesus has redeemed this man! The blood of Jesus has atoned for this man's sin! The blood of Jesus has cleansed him!" Tell the demons what the blood of Jesus means. The blood of Jesus is just as alive as it was the moment it was shed on Calvary. Do not let it become a meaningless ritual in your mouth. Tell the devil what the blood is all about!

In another instance, I saw some people ministering deliverance to a man, and they kept swallowing air and burping. They would swallow air and burp, and then swallow more air and burp. I asked him what was going on, and they told me they were helping the man get delivered. They said "We receive the spirits that are in him, and after we have invited his spirits into us then we then burp them out of us." I spent one whole day ministering to a preacher's wife who had practiced that, inviting other people's evil spirits into herself. That is dangerous stuff, and entirely not scriptural.

I've known people who wanted to get rid of an evil spirit and so they stuck a finger down their throat in order to vomit. Now, quite often when people are getting deliverance they might throw up phlegm and mucus, but *very seldom* have I ever seen anyone regurgitate food when they are getting ministry. Anyhow, you don't get deliverance by induced vomiting. This is a fleshly, carnal method and is therefore of no effect.

I want you to see what the Spirit of God is saying to us here. If you do not rely upon the Holy Spirit we will become carnal, fleshly, and will start using fleshly methods trying to get rid of spiritual beings and it cannot be done that way.

Resorting to the
Voice of Demons for Guidance

If you do not depend upon the Holy Spirit to guide you in the ministry of warfare and deliverance you might even find yourself resorting to the help of demon spirits. I know many cases where the deliverance minister fell into the trap of calling upon the evil spirits to guide them and help them with the ministry of deliverance.

For instance, they say "What is your strategy in this person's life?" "Where did you come from," "How long have you been there?" etc. Now when you do that you are depending upon the demons to guide the ministry rather than the Lord! This is why God gave the *discerning of spirits*, so that we will not have to talk to evil spirits, or rely on them for information, but we can get our information from God.

I have been led, on occasions, to command the ruler spirit to name himself. "In the name of Jesus, I command you to name yourself! Speak your name! and come out in Jesus' Name!"

Under the proper authority of Jesus, with the pressure being applied from the Holy Spirit, that evil spirit has to comply. When it does, it is often through the name of the attribute which it manifests: "Lust," or "Anger," or "Murder."

In *Pigs in the Parlor*, the very first demon I cast out of another pastor had to name himself in order to come out. For sixteen years he had suffered continuous headaches. This was the result of a serious head injury. Doctors were unable to offer a solution. Because of the pain, he could not sleep and his nerves were going to pieces. As we began to command the lead demon to name himself, very slowly and in a voice that was scarcely audible, there was one word spoken — "*PAIN*."

That was it. There was no defiling back and forth or conversing. That's all it took! Quoting what happened next:

"Demon of pain, come out of Fred!" Our words were insistent. "In the name of Jesus, come out of him!" Fred's wife must have sensed in her spirit what was about to happen. She grabbed a newspaper off the coffee table and threw it on the floor between Fred's feet. Immediately Fred coughed and threw up two big blobs of phlegm onto the paper. The demon was out! And the pain was gone! Almost five years have passed and Fred is still healed and free from headaches. God had answered our prayers!

Most of the time, however, it is obvious from talking with the candidate prior to ministry what the root spirit is. And when a demon names himself, I am on guard, and test the Holy Spirit for confirmation as to whether this name is legitimate.

Coming against the strongman is when the battle really heats up.

This brings us to another foundational principle. To rely upon evil spirits rather than upon the Lord is a denial that God's help is sufficient. The Holy Spirit is our one supernatural source, not the unclean spirit, because God is a jealous God. Some people do not realize how jealous God is. There is a passage in the Old Testament that tells us that His name is "jealous." Now that's not a sinful kind of jealousy, mind you. But God has a right to His people. He has created us and He has redeemed us.

The Scripture says that God is like a husband to us, and we are the bride of Christ. Jesus is the bridegroom. Now how would a husband or wife feel if their spouse went somewhere else to get their needs met? That spouse will become jealous, and they would have every right to be jealous. God will not permit us to go to any other source other than Himself for wisdom, knowledge, guidance or power. In fact, He says anyone who has done that has committed "spiritual adultery." That is the reason we cannot go to evil spirits for *knowledge* or *wisdom*.

In the 18th chapter of Deuteronomy there is a listing of those things which are considered occult. This list includes "observers of times;" He is talking here about horoscopes and astrology. It mentions "divination," as in water witching or divining metals. He mentions "necromancy," that is communicating with evil spirits. He talks about "witchcraft," which also involves a communication with evil spirits. God says these things are an *abomination* to Him.

In fact He mentions in that context, and tells the Israelites, that this list of occult activities is the reason that He is giving them the land of Canaan. Because those people, the Canaanites who had lived in this land, polluted their land and themselves through seeking the help of demon spirits. That is the reason God took their inheritance away from them, and gave it to Israel. He goes on to say that if Israel were to turn to those things then He would take the land away from them, too! God says that

15

to have communication with evil spirits is an abomination, and a form of spiritual adultery, that incurs the wrath of God.

"But," you say, "this is an exception, I am an exception, and these are unusual circumstances. So I can lay aside what God said." That's what brought King Saul into trouble, remember? His back was to the wall, and he was so ready to hear something from God. But God was not speaking to him. And instead of correcting his relationship with God so that he could hear from Him, he went to the witch of Endor for help. He felt justified in this, because he was under a pressured circumstance and a very difficult situation. We all know what happened to King Saul as a result of his involvement with the witch of Endor. He lost his life. The reality is that there are often things coming up that tempt us to take information from the evil spirits we are combating. But God says "No, don't do it."

If I were to rely on evil spirits to give me information or to give me understanding during a deliverance session, then I would be doing the same thing that a witch does, the same things that a wizard does, or that a necromancer does, or that a consultant with the departed dead does. Therefore, I would be an abomination to the Lord!

If we seek light or wisdom or knowledge from evil spirits we have sought the kingdom of darkness. The Bible says Satan's kingdom is the kingdom of darkness. We are to be translated out of darkness into the kingdom of God's Son, which is a Kingdom of Light. If we are walking with the Lord, we are walking in His light. If you seek understanding from evil spirits then you have sought *light amid darkness.* Jesus said on the sermon on the Mount, if your light (i.e., your spiritual enlightenment) is darkness, how great is that darkness! If the light that you have came from the kingdom of darkness, you may call it "light" but God calls it "darkness."

This brings us to another foundational principle: to rely upon evil spirits rather than upon the Lord is a denial that God's help is sufficient. This is how *mixture* settles into a person's life, where someone might say "I will listen a little to God and a little to evil spirits. And I'm smart enough to sort out the difference between what's true and what's not true." Evil spirits, much like their overlord Satan, mix a little truth among their lies. Sometimes they will even sound like they're in line with the word of God. But let me ask the question, "Does a deceitful, lying spirit ever tell you anything that's true, in order to help you?" No. He's *not* trying to help you, he's trying to deceive you, to distract you and to put you off. His only concern is hindering the person's deliverance. And so he gives you a little bait. When you take the bait, he leads you down a path somewhere else; away from the truth.

So the question becomes, "Is God sufficient?" Is God's wisdom adequate? Are the gifts of the Spirit enough? If God's wisdom and knowledge is not sufficient, then I would rather not be in the deliverance ministry. I would rather not practice deliverance than to rely upon the lies and distortion of evil spirits.

How, Then, Are We to Know the Strategies of the Enemy?

In 2 Kings 6, the king of Syria had a problem. He was coming in battle against God's people Israel, and every time he would meet in secret and counsel with his military leaders, it turned out that the leaders of Israel knew exactly what he was up to. They knew all of his secret plans. So he decided that somebody within his inner circle must be a spy, that there was an informer in his midst.

> Then the king of Syria warred against Israel, and took counsel with his servants, saying, In such and such a place shall be my camp.

And the man of God [*Elisha*] sent unto the king of Israel, saying, Beware that thou pass not such a place; for thither the Syrians are come down.

And the king of Israel sent to the place which the man of God told him and warned him of, and saved himself there, not once nor twice.

Therefore the heart of the king of Syria was sore troubled for this thing; and he called his servants, and said unto them, Will ye not shew me which of us is for the king of Israel?

And one of his servants said, None, my lord, O king: but Elisha, the prophet that is in Israel, telleth the king of Israel the words that thou speakest in thy bedchamber.

How will we then find out what the enemy is up to? How will we know about his wiles, and the deceitful things that he is plotting?

The Scripture says that we will defeat the devil "in his gates." The gates in the Old Testament were where the leaders drew up their plans for battle. The gates of hell are where the kingdom of Satan draws up his strategy and his council of war. Jesus said the "gates of hell" will not prevail against His Church. This means we will defeat the enemy in his very place of counsel and strategy. How can we possibly know the strategy of the enemy? God can tell us! Amen?

Now look in Joshua 9. This occurs when Joshua was moving into the land of Canaan and conquering his enemies. There were Gibeonites that came to deceive Joshua. They pretended that they were from a country far off, because they knew Joshua was conquering all of the land of the Canaanites. So they asked Joshua for an agreement that he would not attack them, to spare them in his conquest. And so they presented their evidence (in paraphrase): "look at our worn-out clothes, we traveled so far that even our clothes are worn out trying to get here." And "when we started out, we had a fresh supply of bread, and look at how moldy our bread is. This proves that we came from a long way away."

> **And Joshua made peace with them, and made a league with them, to let them live: and the princes of the congregation sware unto them.**
>
> Joshua 9:15

Joshua dealt with them in a simplistic way, by questioning the enemy and taking information from them. But, you see, they were *deceivers* and *liars*. As great a man as Joshua was, he did not detect this. He did not discern it because he did not go to God for wisdom and knowledge.

> **So the men of Israel took some of their provisions, and did not ask for the counsel of the Lord.**
>
> Joshua 9:14 (NASB)

That is where they made their mistake. They sought their information from the enemy rather than from God.

Many are making the same error today. They're looking to the enemy and asking *him* to tell them what the strategy is, rather than seeking the counsel of God and asking the Lord to show the ways in which the devil is working. Where the devil (or his demons) is working, he is always a deceiver and liar.

TWELVE REASONS
NOT TO SPEAK TO DEMONS

I have put together a list of 12 reasons why I do not talk to evil spirits. I think this list supports what we have been saying so far, that reliance on the Holy Spirit, and not conversing with the spirits speaking through the deliverance candidate, is the only effective means and sure way to accomplish the great commission of the Lord.

REASON 1

Demons are all liars. Satan is the father of lies, and he is the head of their kingdom. So, nothing they say can be relied upon.

REASON 2

I have access to truth, all truth. The Holy Spirit is the Spirit of Truth, so I don't need information from evil spirits.

REASON 3

God is a jealous God, and I will look to Him alone for wisdom, guidance, knowledge and power.

REASON 4

Talking with demons discourages the use of the gifts of the Holy Spirit. The Spirit says to covet these gifts and Paul encourages us to stir up the gifts of the Holy Spirit, and to desire earnestly the gifts. This is a matter of obedience to the Lord.

REASON 5

Relying upon information coming from demons gives them the right to direct or control the ministry time. You are no longer in control of the ministry, they are.

REASON 6

There is no sound scriptural basis for conversing with demons.

REASON 7

Requiring demons to talk is inconsiderate of the person. It is a very unedifying experience.

REASON 8

I must flee the temptation of pride by boasting that I have talked with demons.

On this point, a few months ago I heard from a man who was in the ministry of deliverance. He claimed he was talking to demons in order to get information from them. They gave him a lot of information about how their hierarchy was set up, what their names were, etc. He felt that *no one* could successfully minister deliverance unless they had this private information that came from the mouth of evil spirits, information that he was now in possession of. He even wrote a book dedicated to the name of the demon who told him all this.

I found out later that he fell into deep deception which led to the breakup of his marriage. Saints, there is a pattern here that we find in the first chapter of Romans. It is that *doctrinal error leads to moral error*. That's the reason we need to keep ourselves free and clear of every curse of deception. People who get into doctrinal deception soon fall into immorality and sexual sin. That's the pattern; one kind of deception leads to the other kind of deception.

REASON 9

I flee from the lure that I have gained secret knowledge, or spiritual information from demons.

REASON 10

Conversing with demons is not necessary to gain a person's deliverance. We have ministered successfully to thousands of people without talking to evil spirits. Praise the Lord, the gifts of the Spirit work!

REASON 11

Speaking to demons delays or defeats the process of deliverance, which is their goal.

REASON 12

Quoting demons does not build faith. Faith comes by hearing and by quoting the word of God.

The gift of *discerning of spirits* makes speaking with evil spirits totally unnecessary. We need to exercise and cultivate our faith that God has given what we need to effectively minister deliverance.

THE OPERATION OF THE GIFT OF KNOWLEDGE

I want to talk to you now about the specific operation of some of the gifts of the Spirit.

Sometimes the gift of *discerning of spirits* is confused with the operation of the gift of *knowledge*. Many times these two gifts operate so closely in conjunction with one another that it may be difficult to separate one entirely from the other. There will be times that they overlap.

The word of *knowledge* is an understanding of facts that we could not know ourselves; a disclosure of certain facts that were hidden from our own understanding. Sometimes when we are ministering deliverance,

God gives *words of knowledge* where He tells us facts about this person that they themselves may not even know. It may have been something that took place when they were still in their mother's womb or when they were being born.

As an example, I remember on one occasion we were ministering to a boy who had brain damage. He said that he was not able to function in his mind as thoroughly as he should be able to, as a normal person would. So he had spent two extra years studying to graduate from high school, he was now 20 years of age, and he had no plans to attend college because of learning difficulties.

As we began to minister to him, God showed us this was indeed caused by an evil spirit that came in when he was being born. The picture we got in our mind was of an umbilical cord being wrapped around his neck and him being strangled at birth. That deficiency of oxygen caused damage to his brain, and the trauma of that event allowed a demon to enter, and that has been his problem ever since.

So, armed with this word of *knowledge*, we commanded the spirit of *oxygen deficiency* to come out of him. Immediately he began to gasp for breath. As he threw his head back gasping for breath, his face turned blue, and in a few moments he was delivered. God healed him so much so that a few months later he wrote to tell us that he was now applying for college as his mind was functioning well. He was able to proceed with higher education. This is an example of the operation of a *word of knowledge*.

I remember another instance where we were ministering to a woman, and the Lord told us quite clearly that she had, in her past, had an abortion. We did not know this woman, and had only been with her for a few moments when God told us about the abortion. Now abortion is a sin; it is a sin that God will forgive. But she *did not know* abortion was a sin, and thus, she would not have known to confess it specifically as murder. So when we led her in prayer and commanded the spirit of *abortion* to come out of her, the demonic spirit actually materialized. It formed in her throat, and the pressure became so intense that the blood vessels actually burst in her neck and her face from the pressure.

As the spirit materialized, it flew out of her mouth and plopped into a wastebasket sitting in front of her. We all looked in the wastebasket and there we saw a perfectly formed embryo, the size and appearance of a baby that would be about 2 1/2 to 3 months in the womb. **That demon of abortion materialized when it came out of her!** Following this, the spirit of *murder* also materialized, and it came out of her mouth as a spot of bright red blood about the size of a silver dollar and fell into the wastebasket. So there is an example of the *word of knowledge*. She received her deliverance because God gave us facts about her that we had no way of knowing. She would never have known to confess this act of abortion as sin, and we would have been unaware of its presence. Once we knew of the sin, we could use the gift of *discerning of spirits* to call out the spirits of *abortion* and *murder*. (I should caution you at this point about getting wrapped up in manifestations. Most deliverance sessions are not as wild as this one was!)

As shown, the gift of *knowledge* and the *discerning of spirits* sometimes work together, as allied gifts of the Spirit. I remember a very clear instance of that. We had a lady come to us for ministry with a back problem. She had been driving in her car and while shifting gears, something was displaced in her back. She went to a doctor and had her back x-rayed, and the doctor told her that she had a double curvature of the spine, something she had apparently since birth. As a result of her spine not being straight, it had caused a certain weakness which was the reason something went out in her back. She had been suffering that way for about a week, when she managed to climb out of bed and to come see us for prayer.

There were two of us pastors that day to minister to her, and as we began to pray for her back, God showed me a vision (sometimes the word of *knowledge* comes in the form of a vision). In this vision, I saw a birthday cake, a white cake with red lettering on top of it which spelled the number 32. I asked her if a birthday cake with the number 32 meant anything to her, and she said that within three months she was turning 32 years of age. I took that to mean the Lord was pointing to an event of some kind that had occurred around the time of her birth, and specifically three months prior to her being born.

Just then, the other pastor who was with me said that, as we were praying and seeking the Lord, God gave him, through the *discerning of spirits*, a revelation that her problem was rooted in a "spirit of rejection."

So we put the two words from the Lord together, the word of *knowledge* and the *discerning of spirits*, and determined that this woman had a *spirit of rejection* that had entered her while she was still in her mother's womb, three months before she was born. So we proceeded with this information and cast out the *spirit of rejection* from her spine and immediately her spine straightened. That evening, when she returned home, her husband looked at her and he knew something had happened to her. He said "you are taller than you used to be." So he measured her and found out that she had increased 2 inches in height as result of the straightening of her spine. When the demonic spirit of rejection had left her body, she was instantly healed!

The rest of this story is a fascinating confirmation of the vision the Lord had shown us, along with the knowledge and discerning that went with it. Her mother was still living, so she asked her mother if there was any possibility of her having been rejected while in the womb. Her mother admitted that she did not want her daughter to be born, and in fact climbed on top of a dresser and jumped off several times trying to abort the baby. This took place *three months* prior to birth.

So there it was; a perfect illustration of how these gifts of the spirit operate in connection with one another.

The Operation of
the Gift of Discerning of Spirits

The *discerning of spirits* is supernatural insight into the spirit realm. Note that it does not say the gift of "discernment," but the gift of the "discerning of spirits." It's not a general discernment of all things, but it is a limited discerning in relation to evil spirits. It is very valuable to discern spirits, and let me give you some of the purposes of this gift.

Discloses the Presence of Evil Spirits

This gift will disclose the presence and operation of evil spirits.

Looking back, I can see that God provided the resources that I needed for the ministry of deliverance. He knew from the day He baptized me in the Holy Spirit that the emphasis He was going to give me was in the area of deliverance. I didn't know it, but God did. Immediately upon my baptism in the Holy Spirit, God began to equip me. As mentioned at the outset, God equips us for the ministry we have before us.

So the very next day after I received the baptism in the Holy Spirit, which happened in a Full Gospel Businessman's meeting in Denver, Colorado, I was asked to sit on the stage and give my testimony. After I finished my testimony, they asked me to remain on the platform for a while. As I looked toward the back of the room from the platform, I saw a group of hippies that the businessmen had invited into the meeting in the hopes that they would be saved. Three of them stood up and started to head toward the platform. Just at that moment, I knew something was wrong. I turned to the man sitting next to me and I said, "Look! that fellow has a demon in him!" And the man looked at me and said, "Oh, you must have the discerning of spirits." Now I had not studied the gifts of the Holy Spirit, I didn't know what that was. So I said to the man, "well I don't know what I've got, but I know what he's got!"

God was equipping us from the very beginning.[1]

And in that same meeting God gave Ida Mae the *gift of faith* for deliverance. She stood up in the middle of the audience, when the three men were on the platform trying to interrupt the meeting, and she rebuked the demons out of those men. She had only experienced the baptism of the Holy Spirit for two weeks, and she had never been in a meeting like this. She had never seen anything like this, and was normally a quiet person who avoided the attention of others. But in that meeting, she stood up and started rebuking demons! And when she did, all three hippies hit the floor at the same time, flat on their backs: *boom, boom, boom*!

It is good to know what is going on in the spiritual realm.

DISTINGUISHES BETWEEN THE OPERATION OF EVIL SPIRITS AND THE HOLY SPIRIT

Many times evil spirits pose as angels of light. Remember the damsel in Acts 16 who followed Paul around the city? She said "These men are servants of the Most High God." Take notice that what she was saying was true. But there was something wrong with it and Paul knew it was not the Spirit of God. We are told it was a spirit of *divination* and Paul cast it out of her. It was a false religious spirit.

Some people get into spiritual things and think it's the Holy Spirit, when in reality it is an evil spirit. We were once in a meeting where we were praying for people at the front of the auditorium. As one sister approached the front of the room, Ida Mae whispered in my ear "the Lord says do not lay hands on this woman. Don't lay hands on her." Ida Mae operated in a powerful gift of *discerning of spirits*, so I knew something

---

1   To learn about the baptism in the Holy Spirit, and the impact this experience had on the Hammond's deliverance ministry, read their testimony in the booklet called *Promoted by God*. Impact Christian Books, 2012.

was not right. It turns out this woman had a false religious spirit in her. As she came up to the front, the anointing of the Holy Spirit was so strong that she went into a religious gyration; she began to shake and tremble. Now, a lot of people have these kind of seizures, and they think it's the Holy Spirit. In fact, she had been in meetings where people had told her that this was the Holy Spirit! So, she thought that when she went into those seizures that it was the Spirit of God falling on her. But God told us it was a demon — a religious spirit.

So we told her what God had shown us and offered to cast it out of her. She was so sweet and teachable, and she immediately said "yes!" She said she had been confused about this recurring spiritual experience, as there was no fruit in it; there was no blessing or peace in it either. So we ministered to her and the spirit came out of her. Then God said it was all right to lay hands on her for prayer.

HELPS US DETERMINE
WHETHER A PROBLEM IS DEMONIC OR PHYSICAL

A lot of problems may be physical rather than spiritual, or they may be *both*. Jesus found that many physical problems had demonic roots and He treated them as such, including blindness, deafness, fever, epilepsy, torment, vexation, insanity, infirmity — all were the result of evil spirits in those cases. We have also discovered the same thing, that evil spirits are often behind sicknesses, including allergies, tumors, high blood pressure, diabetes, and so on. Many of those things can be the result of the operation of evil spirits, and when identified as such and cast out, the sickness lifts. But on the other hand, we *cannot* say that all physical problems are due to demons.

As an example, I had a woman who persistently called me over months from long distance, and every time she called she said she was tormented by demons and she needed deliverance. It was always the same spirits she needed deliverance from: she would say she needed deliverance from *smoking* and from *gluttony*. "I can't seem to stay off cigarettes," she would say, "I stay off a day or two and then I go back and here I am demonized again. Oh brother Frank, will you cast out that nicotine demon out of me!" Also, she would admit, "It seems like I just keep eating, I raid the refrigerator at night." Here I had visions of her being extremely overweight, but I asked her, "how much overweight are you, sister?" She said "I weigh 90 pounds." I was shocked. But she was still troubled by what she thought was a spirit of *gluttony* that would cause her to get up the middle of the night and eat.

Finally, I said "Sister, there is something else going on, and I don't know what it is, but I'm going to pray and seek the Lord's wisdom, so that I can discern what the problem is in your life."

As I was praying one day, I said "Lord, what about this sister?" The Lord spoke to my spirit and said she has a physical condition called *hypoglycemia*. Hypoglycemia!

I found out that a lot of the symptoms of hypoglycemia are identical to schizophrenia. I called her and told her this and she did not much like that word. I could tell by the response I got over the phone that she just wanted her demons cast out. But when there was no devil to cast out, and she had to believe God for a physical healing, along with regulating her diet, she was not so happy. You see a person who has hypoglycemia has low blood sugar. When their blood sugar gets low they begin to act and feel listless and weak, and so they need a charge which they can get from eating. Hence she would raid the refrigerator. Or, you can get the same charge from drinking alcohol or smoking cigarettes; these give a surge in blood sugar. So this was the reason the Lord showed us that she had these cravings, or what she called "gluttony;" it wasn't demons that were driving her, but it was hypoglycemia. And this was a physical problem.

Not shortly thereafter, when I returned from a ministry trip, I spoke to my associate pastor and he said that this lady had called, not for ministry, but to give a victory report. God had healed her, she said, of her hypoglycemia and she had regulated her diet according to the wisdom God had given her and everything was now fine. She was out of the pit she had been in for so many years.

So it's good to know what is going on the spiritual realm. The gift of *discerning of spirits* can lead us to the true source of a problem, be it spiritual or physical.

GUIDES THE DELIVERANCE MINISTER
THROUGH THE PROCESS OF DELIVERANCE

In a practical sense, when the gift of discerning is in operation, it's just like a "knowing." To me, most of the time, I just know what demons are in operation, as if my spirit is programmed with the Truth.

When we minister deliverance to an individual, we should not rely upon manifestations as our guide, but rather the Holy Spirit. He should be the guide as we work with someone through a deliverance. We may feel the Lord urging us to cast out various spirits, as He administers the *discerning of spirits*, and yet we do not see any manifestation. Did we not hear the Spirit correctly?

For instance, as I begin ministering, I may become aware of the presence of a specific spirit, through the Holy Spirit's urging. As I call out this specific demon, I don't see any manifestation; I don't get any witness in my spirit that a demon has left. But I get another discerning, for a second spirit. Instead of hammering on that first spirit, I call for the second spirit to come out. God is not the author of confusion, and I have to trust in faith that He is leading me when I am praying deliverance for somebody. If we were not through with one demon, He would not have given me the name of the second spirit. So I'll call that one to come out, and I may *still not see* any manifestation. Just like the first spirit, I may not get a witness in my spirit that the demon has come out. And as the Lord leads, I call another spirit, and another spirit; sometimes I go through 25 or 30 demons and as far as looking at anything in the natural, nothing has happened. But when I get to the 30th demon, then something breaks and all 30 come out the same time, "Blah!" That's the value of letting the Lord lead the battle. It takes the sweat out of it. It takes the strain out of it. You flow with the Holy Spirit, and let Him lead the battle. He knows the proper sequence to unlock a person's bondage.

When you are ministering to groups it works the same way. Sometimes in a group ministry the Lord will have me personalize a deliverance for somebody in the audience. We'll be calling the spirits generally out of everybody in attendance and there may be someone there that the Holy Spirit wants delivered of a specific thing.

As an example, I was ministering in the Los Angeles area once, and we were having a powerful group deliverance session with about 600 people in attendance. That night, as I was ministering from the platform, I received a discernment that I had never received before: *sickle cell anemia*. And so I called for the spirit of *sickle cell anemia* to come out of someone, not knowing who it was for. There was a precious girl about 18 or 19 years of age and she screamed out at that precise moment. It was there! That demon was present in her. If I had followed a prescribed list, like the demon groupings in *Pigs in the Parlor*, and had just worked through the names of demons listed in Chapter 20, that girl would not have received her deliverance that night, because it doesn't have *sickle cell anemia* in that list! I had never called for that spirit before.

So if you are tuned into the Spirit of the Lord and you are following the discernment that the Lord gives, you can be led like this. He knows what challenges people have far better than I ever would. So, when I prepare to minister, I say, "God I don't know what these people need, You need to show me by Your Spirit. You tell me what demons are present. I don't want to follow a prescribed list, Lord. I want to know from You what devils to come against and in what order."

Enables Us to Distinguish Between a False Prophet and a True Prophet

There are men and women that come as a wolf in sheep's clothing; this is a hard lesson to learn. In the 13th chapter of Acts, it tells us about a sorcerer whose name was Elymas. Paul received a powerful discernment on him such that he called Elymas a "child of the devil," and an "enemy of everything that is right." He discerned the spirits that were motivating that man, this sorcerer.

I was asked one time to lead a small group meeting, where a new member was going to be announced. This new member was a businessman who had just moved into the area, and the leader of the small group told me that he was baptized in the Holy Spirit, and an on-fire Christian businessman who wanted to use his business resources to spread the news of what the Lord was doing through that small group. Sounded good, right?

But as he walked in the door, the Spirit of God spoke to me and said "he is a wolf in sheep's clothing." That was a powerful word; I still remember it to this day. And before that meeting was over, the wolf nature had showed itself in a very demonstrable way. In fact he was such a problem in that town that the local people eventually ran him off. It's good to walk in the Spirit of the Lord and to know what's going on in the spiritual realm.

Allows Us to Discern the Strongman over Families, Churches, Cities and Nations[2]

The Holy Spirit wants to disclose who the strong ruler spirits are over nations. We were ministering in a part of Canada once, and before the meeting we were on our knees praying, and the Lord said to us quite

---

2   For more information, see the Hammond's book on spiritual warfare in the heavens, entitled *The Saints at War*. Impact Christian Books, 2013.

clearly that the ruling spirit over that area was a "wilderness spirit, wild and unrestrained in nature." It was that spirit that had attracted most of the people to move to that area. It was closely aligned with the spirit of *escapism*. We were able to better minister to that audience as we knew the way to break through the spirits that ruled over that geographic area.

When Ida Mae and I went to other countries in Europe, God has shown us, through the *discerning of spirits*, what the ruling spirits are over various countries. The same is true of cities. God has shown us the ruling spirit over cities here in the United States. This is information given to us for a purpose — that we might *bind* those ruler spirits so that the Lord's Spirit can fully shine into an area and the Gospel can have its effect on the hearts and minds of those living there. It is a very rewarding and fruit-bearing spiritual battle to fight when you know that eternity is at stake.

It also can be true that, when ministering to an entire family, we may learn of a ruling demonic spirit over the lineage, a strongman. Knowing this ruling spirit may allow us to unlock an entire family's bondage. In some cases, this breakthrough can have the effect of setting a future lineage free from a source of demonic bondage. So we must be faithful to listen to the Lord and receive instruction from Him.[3]

3   For more information on family or generational issues, see *The Breaking of Curses* by Frank and Ida Mae Hammond. Impact Christian Books, 2013.

MY PRAYER FOR YOU

There is a purpose in impartation, as described in both the Old and New Testaments. The Lord has given us, through our deliverance ministry, the gift of *wisdom*, the gift of *knowledge*, the gift of *discerning of spirits* and the gift of *faith*. Those are the primary gifts that God has given to us to operate in the ministry of deliverance. Since you are a deliverance people, and you are part of the warring church of Jesus Christ, the Church against which the gates of hell will not prevail, I feel strongly that you need these same gifts active in your life.

In the closing section of this message, I believe God wants these same four gifts of the Holy Spirit imparted to you such that you may rise to a whole new level of spiritual warfare and ministry in deliverance. We are going to pray that you might move to *an even greater* level of effectiveness in defeating Satan's forces, his evil spirits and in particular, his strongmen.

I would prefer to lay hands on you individually and pray over you, even prophesy over you, and ask the Holy Spirit to impart the gifts mentioned above into your life. But I am going to trust the Holy Spirit to bring this impartation to completion in your life as we pray this prayer together, and thereby impart to you the gifts of *wisdom*, *knowledge*, the *discerning of spirits*, and *faith*. This is for a purpose, so that you might be able to minister to those in need around you, including your immediate family, others in your church, and those in your community.

This is no mere formality. This is the truth of God's word being applied to your life. Just as when the anointing came on Aaron, the oil flowed from the top of his head down his garments even to the hem of his robe, so I ask the Lord to anoint you with His precious gifts right now. We are going to pray for you to receive a touch from God, a new measure of his Holy Spirit that you might be empowered from on high. That you will be enabled to do the ministry of God with the very real demonstration of the Holy Spirit's power.

If you have not been baptized in the Holy Spirit, we suggest you pursue this experience first, as it is the foundation for the prayer we are about to pray. With that in mind, let's pray together:

Lord, we pray for all those reading this teaching with a strong desire, that they would sense Your willingness to empower them, and to open new doors to them in order to bring people out of bondage. Let them know Your willingness to equip them, in order to bring the freedom You purchased at the Cross; I pray the release of these gifts so that they might minister to their families, friends, neighbors and those in their community.

As Aaron was anointed, and the anointing flowed down his garments and even to the hem of his robe, covering his entire body, Lord we are asking for the anointing of the Holy Spirit's power to flow upon this reader today, from their head to their feet, that they may be overwhelmed by the loving, refining presence of the Holy Spirit – and become a vessel cleansed and purified for Your glory. May they walk in a powerful and effective manner for your Kingdom.

Lord help them turn away from the weapons of carnality and the flesh, and from whatever man or the enemy seeks to supply, and turn instead to You, honoring You and glorifying You, through the use of the gifts of the Holy Spirit.

In the name of *Jesus*, we now impart the anointing of the Holy Spirit, that this person might move in a demonstration of power of these mighty gifts, and be used as a lighthouse, and as a refuge, to those who are weary, those who are oppressed, those who are tormented and those who are afflicted by the enemy. That troubled souls might find a place of help and peace, and come to know the mighty power of Your delivering Hand. That lost souls might find the anchor of Your hope, Jesus, and flee to the Rock that is higher than they. All this through the personal ministry of those praying this prayer now. I pray now for a touch of the living God; a strengthening and an equipping for this reader's mind, body and soul.

And in the name of *Jesus,* I now impart to whomever is praying this prayer, the gift of *faith*, the gift of *wisdom*, the gift of *knowledge*, and the gift of *discerning of spirits*, for their equipping for the work of God's dear Son.

In the name of *Jesus*, we declare it done! Hallelujah! Let it be done, Lord.

We declare it done in the high and holy name of *Jesus*.

Thank you Jesus, thank you Lord.

Amen!

Parting Words

There was a lady who walked up to me one day, thinking that I can discern spirits at will, and she stood before me and she said, "Brother Hammond, I don't want anything in me that's not of God. I want you to discern me. So, you look at me and you tell me if you see any demons in me."

So I studied her very carefully: I looked at her from the tip of her toes right up to the top of her head, and I said, "Well, yes Sister, I do see something." And her eyes got big and she said nervously, "What is it Brother Hammond, what is it?"

I said, "I see Jesus in you."

People think that, because Ida Mae and I are in the ministry of deliverance, that we are constantly looking at people and discerning what demons they might have. The truth of the matter is that when I look at people who are among the family of God, I only see one thing: I see Jesus. I do not see rooms full of demonized people, I see "Jesus people!"

Jesus said not to get obsessed with demons. We are to pay attention to demons, because they are real, and we have to get rid of them, so we can become more effective in our walk with Jesus. But there's a difference between dealing with demons and being obsessed with them. In Luke 10:20, when the seventy came back celebrating their victories over Satan and his evil spirits, Jesus said:

> … **rejoice not, that the spirits are subject unto you; but rather rejoice, because your names are written in heaven.**

That is the foremost thing. People often wonder that so much of our energy and time is spent in the ministry of deliverance and yet we say to people "be more Jesus-conscious than you are demon-conscious." It is really all about Jesus. Amen? Amen!

APPENDIX
MARK 16:9–20

There has been a belief (or rumor) that Mark 16:9–20, and that version of the Great Commission, was not included in the original ancient Bible texts. We have carefully researched this, and have found this not to be the case. Mark's version of the Great Commission includes the command to *cast out demons*, to *speak in new tongues* and to *heal the sick*, much like Philip (the Evangelist) did in Acts 8. The fact is that, in many of the ancient manuscripts that date to the same period of time, Mark's Great Commission is there! Also, certain Church fathers refer to this specific passage in Mark 16 as early as the second century, before the Gospel of Mark was even compiled.

There are five ancient manuscripts that have formed our Bible. Each of these documents date to the 5th Century A.D. (the 400s A.D.). They are the "unicals," because the text was written in capital letters. These five manuscripts are as follows:

1. The **Vatican Manuscript** held in the Vatican Library. This manuscript is often considered the most important one, although it is an incomplete rendering of the Bible. Specifically, it is missing Genesis 46:28, Hebrews 9:14 to the end, and all of Timothy, Titus, and Revelation. This document is also missing Mark 16:9–20. However, interestingly, the scribe *left a space for these verses*. This strongly suggests something was written in Mark 16 but the scribe did not copy it either due to an oversight or a theological position.

2. The **Sinaitic Manuscript** or codex. This manuscript was discovered by Constantin Tischendorf at St. Catherine's Monastery on Mt. Sinai. As with the Vatican Manuscript, Mark 16:9–20 is omitted.

3. ***The Alexandrian Manuscript*** (or Codex Alexandrinus). This is the first of the five manuscripts found with Mark 16:9–20, so these verse are in the manuscript.

4. ***The codex Ephraem***. This ancient manuscript, dating from the 400s also, contains Mark 16:9–20.

5. ***The codex Bexae***. This manuscript is not as highly valued as the others, but it is considered an excellent resource for our Bible. Mark 16:9–20 appears in this version also.

In addition, all the later unicals, a number of Old Latin authorities, the Vulgate, and many other versions contain these passages from Mark.[4]

The earliest reference to Mark 16:9–20 was by Justin Martyr around 160 A.D. And Irenaeus, in his work "Against Heresies" from around 184 A.D., cites Mark 16:19 and reveals that *Mark was the author*. Why is this dating important? Because these references are *more than 100 years older* than the earliest complete manuscript of Mark. It proves that Mark's full version of the Great Commission was in existence very early on. This passage simply could not have been inserted by a rogue scribe or monk.

It is clear to us, that Mark 16:9–20 was actively in use by Church fathers prior to the compilation of all five of the "unicals" mentioned above. It is specifically because of the *explosive* nature of these verses, that they were called into question. These verses link the power of the baptism in the Holy Spirit, along with the casting out of demons and the healing of the sick, to the Great Commission as spoken by Jesus Himself. This, therefore, was a *serious threat* to the enemy. Spiritual forces were at work to deny Mark's Great Commission its proper place in the Bible.

These powerful verses from Mark are presented below:

4 "How We Got the Bible," Third Edition revised and expanded, by Neil R. Lightfoot: Baker Books, Copyright 1963, 1988, 2003.

And He said to them, "Go into all the world and preach the gospel to all creation.

These signs will accompany those who have believed: in My name they will cast out demons, they will speak with new tongues; they will pick up serpents, and if they drink any deadly poison, it will not hurt them; they will lay hands on the sick, and they will recover."

(NASB)

FRANK HAMMOND BOOKS & E-BOOKS

Pigs in the Parlor

A handbook for deliverance from demons and spiritual oppression, patterned after the ministry of Jesus Christ. With over 1 million copies in print worldwide, and translated into more than a dozen languages, *Pigs in the Parlor* remains the authoritative book on the subject of deliverance.

9780892280278

Study Guide: *Pigs in the Parlor*

Designed as a study tool for either individuals or groups, this guide will enable you to diagnose your personal deliverance needs, walk you through the process of becoming free, and equip you to set others free from demonic torment. Includes questions and answers on a chapter-by-chapter basis as well as new information to further your knowledge of deliverance.

9780892281992

A Manual for
Children's Deliverance

A book to help parents minister to children, and a valuable tool for them to learn how to set their children free from spiritual bondages. Topics include: Jesus' ministry to children, when the womb is unsafe, methods for ministering to children, occult infiltration of childhood, a child's imagination, and more.

9780892280780

Confronting Familiar Spirits
Counterfeits to the Holy Spirit

A person can form a close relationship with an evil spirit, willfully or through ignorance, for the purposes of knowledge or gain. When a person forms a relationship with an evil spirit, he then "has a familiar spirit." Familiar spirits operate as counterfeits to the gifts of the Holy Spirit.

9780892280179

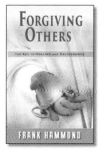

Forgiving Others:
The Key to Healing & Deliverance

Unforgiveness is an obstacle to our walk with Jesus, and can be a roadblock to the deliverance and freedom of our souls. Frank Hammond explains the spiritual truths regarding the necessity of forgiveness and the blessings of freedom which result.

9780892280766

FRANK HAMMOND BOOKS & E-BOOKS

PRAISE:
A WEAPON OF WARFARE & DELIVERANCE

Praise is a powerful weapon in deliverance and spiritual warfare. What happened when David began to play on his harp and sing praise to his God? The evil spirit departed from King Saul. As you praise the Lord, things begin to happen in the unseen realm. A demon cannot exist in that atmosphere — he simply cannot function.

9780892283859

OBSTACLES TO DELIVERANCE:
WHY DELIVERANCE SOMETIMES FAILS

Why does deliverance sometimes fail? This is, in essence, the same question raised by Jesus' first disciples, when they were unable to cast out a spirit of epilepsy. Jesus gave a multi-part answer which leads us to take into account the strength of the spirit confronted and the strategy of warfare employed. 9780892282036

SPIRITUAL WARFARE
FOR LOST LOVED ONES

Through spiritual warfare, intercessory prayer, and the ministry of love, we are creating the best possible environment around a loved one to come to know Jesus. Frank Hammond says, "Don't let your family or friends go without *resistance*. Get in the spiritual battle, fight for your loves ones!" 9780892283842

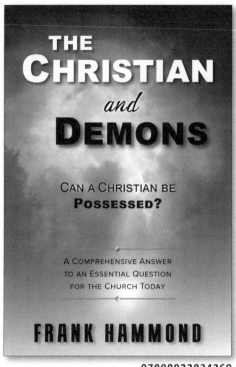

97808922834269

THE CHRISTIAN & DEMONS

CAN A CHRISTIAN BE POSSESSED? *LIKE IN THE MOVIES?*

This is one of the most challenging and controversial issues in the Body of Christ today. The uncertainty surrounding this issue creates an obstacle to the greater move of the Holy Spirit taking place on earth. In this concise teaching, Frank Hammond answers the most pressing questions about the deliverance ministry, and whether it applies to Christians today...

- HOW CAN A CHRISTIAN, WITH THE HOLY SPIRIT DWELLING IN HIM OR HER, HAVE A DEMON?

- HOW DOES DEMONIC ACTIVITY COMPARE TO WHAT I HAVE SEEN ON TV OR IN MOVIES?

- ISN'T THIS A MINISTRY FOR REALLY MESSED UP PEOPLE, BEFORE THEY ACCEPT JESUS?

- AREN'I MOST OF MY PROBLEMS PHYSICAL, NOT SPIRITUAL?

- DOES THE BIBLE ACTUALLY SAY CHRISTIANS CAN BE *POSSESSED*?

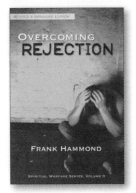

OVERCOMING REJECTION

Frank Hammond addresses the all-too-common root problem of *rejection* and the *fear of rejection* in the lives of believers, and provides steps to be set free. Learn how past experiences can influence our actions, and how we can be made whole. Discover the various causes of rejection, including abuse by parents, peer rejection, marital rejection, Church related rejection, and others.

9780892281053 BOOK OR E-BOOK

AUDIO CD: REJECTION – CAUSE & SOLUTION

In this practical teaching, Frank Hammond highlights the common causes of rejection in our lives, and explains how it can begin as early as in the womb. Frank explains his own battles with rejection which began early in childhood and affected his adult years as a young pastor.

9780892283941 CD

AUDIO CD: BREAKING DEMONIC STRONGHOLDS

The enemy of our souls has a master plan for each one of us, and it includes the wound of *rejection*. Everyone has to deal with it. The good news is that Jesus provided the overwhelming power to heal our personality — through deliverance, the casting out of demons. This breakthrough teaching by Frank and Ida Mae Hammond was presented in Pigs in the Parlor. Frank Hammond explains demonic strongholds through a common pattern of spirits.

9780892283637 CD

THE BREAKING OF CURSES

The Bible refers to curses over 230 times, and seventy sins that cause curses are listed in Scripture. Curses are just as real today as they were in Biblical times. This book shows what curses are and how you may deliver yourself and your family from them. Discussion includes generational curses, cursed objects, curses spoken over people, authority–figure curses, witchcraft, and steps to breaking curses. **9780892281091 BOOK OR E-BOOK**

DVD VIDEO: BREAKING CURSES

Through the Name of Jesus, we have the authority to cast out the demons that are behind the power of curses. At the end of this DVD, Frank Hammond conducts deliverance ministry to break the curses in people's lives. **9780892282289 DVD**

LEARN THE BLESSINGS OF GODLY SOUL-TIES & HOW TO BREAK UNGODLY SOUL-TIES...

"Here at last is a thorough and theologically sound treatment of a little understood subject"

- from the Foreword by **Frank Hammond**

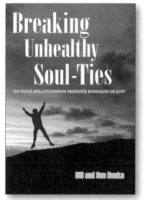

BREAKING UNHEALTHY SOUL-TIES

Unhealthy soul-ties involve the control of one individual over another, and can be a difficult block to spiritual freedom. Some relationships are healthy and bring blessings into our lives; other types of relationships can bring demonic bondage to our souls. This book assists the reader in diagnosing both healthy and unhealthy relationships, and offers positive steps to personal freedom.

BILL & SUE BANKS, **9780892281398**

SOUL TIES

Frank Hammond's booklet on Soul Ties. Good soul ties include marriage, friendship, parent to child, and between sincere Christians. Bad soul ties include those formed from fornication, evil companions, perverted family ties, with the dead, and demonic ties through the Church.

HAMMOND, **9780892280162**

AUDIO CD: FREEDOM FROM DEMONIC SOUL TIES (2 CDs)

Frank Hammond teaches on healthy and unhealthy soul ties in this Audio series, including ministry at the end for breaking demonic soul ties in our lives.

HAMMOND, **9780892283613 CD**

On Defeating Sexual Strongholds

Repercussions from Sexual Sins
Frank Hammond

The sexual revolution has impacted our nation, our church and our family. Promiscuity, nudity, pornography and sexual obscenities are now commonplace. The inevitable consequence of defilement is the loss of fellowship with a holy God. We can break free from the bondage of sexual sin! **9780892282050**

The Marriage Bed
Frank Hammond

Can the marriage bed be defiled? Or, does anything and everything go so long as husband and wife are in agreement with their sexual activities? Drawing from God's emphasis on purity and holiness in our lives, this booklet explains how to avoid perverse sexual demonic activity in a home. **9780892281862**

9780892280575

Ministering to Abortion's Aftermath
Wm & Sue Banks

The world has sold us a life without consequences. As a result, millions of women have had abortions. Those who are tormented by pain and regret of this decision have access to the throne of God to receive His mercy and love. They also have access to His mighty delivering power. Read a dozen real-life stories of women who have found deliverance and freedom from the burdens and bondage associated with abortion. Learn how their triumph can be yours!

Deliverance from Childlessness

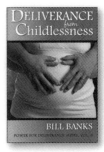

Are you aware that the Bible has a lot to say about childlessness? Or, that demonic spirits can – in some cases – prevent childbirth? This book ministers to women and men with truths to overcome barrenness. Find the first real hope for childless couples; because for some, there is *a spiritual block preventing conception*.

Bill & Susan Banks

9780892280377

BOOKS ON DELIVERANCE FOR THE FAMILY AND FOR CHILDREN

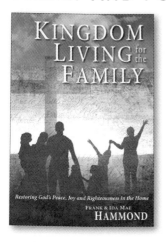

KINGDOM LIVING
FOR THE FAMILY
FRANK HAMMOND

Families today are hurting and broken as never before. Many are frustrated by the cycle of strife and discord between husbands and wives, and between parents and children. Frank and Ida Mae Hammond reveal God's strong desire to heal and deliver the family, and they present a realistic plan to bring its members into a place of security within God's will. **9780892281008**

COMFORT FOR THE WOUNDED SPIRIT
FRANK HAMMOND

A message of hope and healing for those who are downtrodden, bruised, crushed and broken by calamity. The Hammonds show how deliverance from unclean spirits and the healing of inner wounds are separate, yet companion, ministries. **9780892280773**

DELIVERANCE FOR CHILDREN & TEENS

A practical handbook for ministering deliverance to children. The material in this book is arranged to help parents diagnose their children's problems and find solutions for destructive behavior. Includes a discussion of generational or hereditary issues, the role of discipline in the home, ministering to adopted children, and help for teens. **9780892280346** BILL BANKS

THE LITTLE SKUNK:
A CHILDREN'S INTRODUCTION TO DELIVERANCE

A children's story book! For the child to read with a parent to understand the subject of deliverance without fear. Includes color illustrations to accompany the story, and assistance at the end for the parent to pray with the child. *Deliverance need not be frightening if properly presented.*

9780892281206 SUE BANKS

FRANK HAMMOND
ON LIVING AGGRESSIVE SPIRITUAL LIVES

THE PERILS OF PASSIVITY   9780892281602

There is a purpose in God for each of us - and it is not passivity! Passivity is a foe to all believers in Christ – it can even block deliverance. Deliverance is not a final goal, it is only a sub-goal on the way to fulfill God's purpose in life. Without an aggressive stance against the enemy, we fall back into passivity, and our service to the Lord is hindered. God said to Pharaoh, "Let my people go *that they may serve Me*" (Exod. 7:16).

THE SAINTS AT WAR   9780892281046

There is a war on for your family, your city and your nation. Christians are in conflict with demons and territorial spirits. This is nothing new... the prophet Daniel confronted the "prince of Persia" when interceding for the captive people of God. Now learn how you, too, can be involved in fighting for your family, city and nation, and in doing so, change the course of history.

AUDIO CD: BINDING THE STRONGMAN

There are strongmen in the demonic kingdom, "ruler" spirits over individuals, families, cities and nations. Scripture reveals that there are also Godly, angelic rulers assigned over every family and nation. God has an army. He is the Lord of Hosts, the "Lord of Armies."

9780892283644 CD

Impact Christian Books

Website: WWW.IMPACTCHRISTIANBOOKS.COM

Phone Order Line: (314)-822-3309

Address: IMPACT CHRISTIAN BOOKS
332 Leffingwell Ave. #101
Kirkwood, MO 63122 USA